A Simple Nest

a holistic approach

to organizing your space

A SIMPLE NEST

ISBN-13 978-1-7347615-0-4
ISBN-10 1-7347615-0-4

Cover and Interior Design: Stone Ridge Books

www.asimplenest.com

A Simple Nest

a holistic approach
to organizing your space

Liz Ryan & Kari Kim

DEDICATION

We dedicate this book to our clients, who have opened their doors to us, allowed us to come into their homes, turn them upside down and transform their worlds. Thank you for teaching us the importance of patience and compassion when letting go and moving forward.

ACKNOWLEDGEMENTS

With grateful hearts, we extend a huge thank you to our friend Nikki for helping us bring our stories and lessons together on paper. Your guidance and expertise are a true gift!

To our delightful and talented friend Blair, thank you for being the extra pair of eyes we needed and for providing us with your words of encouragement.

And to our families, we can never thank you enough for believing in us and supporting us as we pursue our dream. Through your patience and encouragement, we have been able to change lives, one nest at a time.

CONTENTS

INTRODUCTION

J ust when we think we have seen it all, the next job proves us wrong. From hoarders and collectors to snakes in garages, dead mice in attic boxes and hidden skeletal remains, we have yet to decide what has challenged us most. And though finding bags of cash and rare gemstones keeps work intriguing, it is the mid-century love letters and French erotica that keep our job fascinating! Regardless, every new project brings a sense of exhilaration that allows us to wake up each day and hit the ground running.

The work in itself is always an adventure, but our clients are what make our job rewarding. Whether we are with them for a day, a week, or on and off for years, we form a connection with them and are grateful they have entrusted us with their most private selves, in their most personal spaces, at their most vulnerable time - a time when they are overwhelmed by physical and mental excess.

Excess breeds chaos and affects every aspect of our lives. The choices we make when we feel overwhelmed not only disrupt relationships and our surroundings, but can impact us in such a negative way that we become blinded as to what our life's purpose is. So, while anxiety, stress, and possibly depression escalate as we try to manage it all, the future generation is right there, on the sidelines, watching.

We wanted to write this book to share the lessons we have learned on our journey to simplify our own lives and the lives of our clients. Our mission is to help you create space and time so that you can begin living your life with intention and purpose. Together, we will eliminate the excess that distracts you from living your best life. Using a holistic approach focusing on the home, the spirit and the earth, we will give you the tools you need to reduce clutter, repurpose old items, donate or recycle your excess goods and save money. You will begin to walk a simpler path, wake up your sense of creativity and explore your passions.

Though we encourage you to surround yourself with the things you love and that inspire you, our philosophy extends much deeper. To obtain the simple lifestyle that so many of us crave, it is imperative to get to the core of the issues that have allowed disorganization, chaos and stress to prevail. Only then can real change endure.

PS. All names have been changed.

I. WHAT IS A SIMPLE NEST?

Give time, give space to sprout your potential.
Awaken the beauty of your heart – the beauty of your spirit.
There are infinite possibilities.
-Amit Ray

Simple is defined as having few parts, not complex or fancy. In turn, a nest is a snug retreat or refuge, a resting place, or home. A Simple Nest unites these two concepts. The result is a home that is calm and nurturing, where less is more. By clearing the physical and mental clutter you can begin living with intention. By surrounding yourself with what you love, what celebrates you and what you truly need, you eliminate the excess in your life that prevents you from living well, living beautifully and living more carefree. That is what creates a simple nest.

II. THE WHEEL

Beware the barrenness of a busy life.
– Socrates

D ay-to-day life can be all consuming. Trying to manage family, home, jobs, extracurricular activities and volunteer work is definitely a balancing act. Hectic lives create tension and lead to oversights, wasted money and conflict. On top of all that, we have excess stuff hovering over us like a big black cloud, robbing us of our joy and taking control of our lives. It is as if we are spinning on a wheel, unable to dismount and catch our breath or embark on a new course. Disheartened, we avoid changing our ways and continue on the same path with the same behavior day after day.

With access to excess at every turn, we make hasty decisions. We have the convenience of prepackaged breakfasts, lunches and dinners, and our latest desire can be delivered to our door within 24 hours. We spend thousands of dollars on books, gadgets and apps for our phones that promise to make life easier and help us feel more in control. Our homes become cluttered and unhealthy, stress seeps into our relationships, and everything suffers. The financial, physical and psychological impact of living in chaos is very real, and we have witnessed the effects far too often.

Early on in our career together, we were hired to empty a property on Sullivan's Island, home to one of Charleston, South Carolina's most beautiful beaches, and would spend six weeks clearing the house from top to bottom. Due to the overwhelming amount of trash and items ruined from weather and mold, we rented a walk-in dumpster (which would end up being replaced two times). One morning, a few weeks into the project, we pulled up to the house to observe a man practically upside down in our dumpster. Not only was he trespassing, but we could see that he had started a pile of wrapping paper, broken picture frames and Christmas decorations. All of the items he was pulling from the dumpster were molded from being stored under the house, and we had found it necessary to wear gloves and masks before we discarded them into the dumpster. He quickly informed us that his name was Danny and that he was one of our client's neighbors. We insisted that the items were contaminated and that we were liable for the dumpster and its contents. Sensing his aggravation, we watched him walk away empty-handed. From that day forward, he would be known as "Dumpster Danny".

A few weeks later, we saw Dumpster Danny and his wife at the estate sale we prepared and hosted for this property. They attended the sale each of the three days we opened it to the public and hauled off loads of merchandise with each visit. Since the point of the sale was to get rid of household goods for our client, we would have greatly appreciated their patronage had their checks not bounced. Lesson learned: cash only at our estate sales from now on.

We were able to coordinate a time to come by Dumpster Danny's home and pickup the cash owed. After ringing the doorbell, we were greeted by Danny's wife and the life-sized Santa they had purchased at our estate sale. What was more amazing than seeing Santa Clause in July was the floor-to-ceiling STUFF that consumed every room of the tiny house. Beyond the realms of their foyer was nothing short of mayhem. Danny and his wife were hoarders. They had wanted the merchandise from the estate sale so badly that they were willing to risk bounced checks and their reputation to get it. Their home was dirty, unsafe and a prison to their desires. It was then that one of the most valuable lessons we would learn hit us right between the eyes. Stuff can control our lives.

The desire to get organized and live simply is now a movement. People are genuinely trying to get their lives in order. In most of our clients' homes, we find at least one book on organizing collecting dust on the bookshelf. We also find closets, attics and garages filled with matching, stacked, utilitarian bins storing paperwork, hand-me-downs and other excess items to go through at a later date. Intentions are good but getting started is too overwhelming.

Living simply does not mean that everything should look perfect and remain tidy at all times. Living simply means gaining control of our lives by reducing what we have to manage. If we want to live differently, deciding to change is first and foremost. Only then can we learn to recognize habits and routines that have prevented us from reaching our goals and fulfilling the vision we have for our lives. As we create room to breathe, our home begins to represent who we are and what we love while offering a warm and welcoming place to find comfort, joy and peace.

The wonderful news is that the simple life we all crave can be achieved by anyone! Just as a mother-to-be "nests" and prepares her home for the arrival of her new little one, following our Simple Nest Process will help prepare you, and your home, for a new way of life. But first, we have come up with a few questions to get the ball rolling. The point of this exercise is to illustrate that all of the organizing in the world will only be a temporary Band-Aid unless we get to the root of the problem. Why? Because life happens, chaos will enter back in, and before we know it, we are right back on that wheel.

1. Why do you shop? The reasons for shopping can be endless, i.e. searching for fulfillment because you are in an unhappy relationship or job; you are in search of the next life changing solution; you can't find the item, or are not sure you have the item, and therefore have to buy another. In many of the families that we have worked with the money wasted on frivolous shopping is phenomenal. Your family's financial health is largely dependent on the choices you make. This is a major reason, if not the number one reason, to begin to recognize your behavior and habits as well as the behaviors and habits of your loved ones.

2. Are activities you commit to a joy or a burden? Are your extracurricular activities taking precious time away from your family? Is your home life suffering as you try to balance it all? It is important to find time to do the things that are meaningful to us outside of work and family. However, stretching ourselves too thin can result in major consequences. Even activities we love can become a burden if we are trying to squeeze them into an already full schedule. With awareness we can learn to recognize that the activity is no longer adding value to our life, and then take steps to create space.

3. Do you volunteer out of desire or obligation? This is difficult because when others do not step up to the plate, we feel we must. Then the project we are volunteering for, meant for good, becomes an added stress. Many of us struggle with the ability to say "no". We see it as a sign of weakness rather than strength. The ability to set limits means you have a strong sense of self. Saying "no" means that you are putting you and your family first and that you do not have the time to do the project justice. Sound familiar? If so, take the time to evaluate the pros and cons of taking on a new project before putting yourself in a situation that will possibly add stress to your life, affect your behavior toward family and friends, affect the outcome of the project for which you are volunteering and most definitely affect your health.

4. Are your kids over-extended? The pressures children face today far exceed what we experienced growing up. School is more demanding, as is the need to perform. The expectations that have been placed on the next generation, whether consciously or unconsciously are immense. These expectations are taking their toll on our youth as depression, anxiety and eating disorders are rising epidemics in our country. Stepping back and evaluating your child's schedule is essential to their wellbeing. Keep the lines of communication open and don't forget to ask them how they feel. As previously mentioned, setting limitations requires courage.

5. Do you try to be a one-man show? Do you try to do it all yourself? Do you think no one else can do it as well you can? Are there able bodies in your home that can pitch in? If you have not learned the art of delegation, you are not only failing yourself, but you are failing your family as well. Lightening your load is a gift to everyone! Not only are you freeing up time to be present and serve the needs of those you love more effectively but you are showing your children that you trust them with important tasks. This teaches them responsibility and the beauty of helping others. Is this always easy? Of course not! Often it would be easier to just do it yourself. Changing behavior takes time, and this not only includes children, but maybe even a spouse who is not used to having additional responsibility.

6. Are you a stacker, stuffer or tucker? Either way you are a procrastinator! Do you have piles around your house that you plan on getting to later? Do you stuff or tuck things here and there? Do you step out of your pants and leave them on the floor to be picked up by someone else? Leaving chores for later that could be done in the moment has consequences. Don't put off doing today what you think can be done tomorrow because tomorrow will bring its own set of needs and to-do's!

7. Do you feel pressure to keep up with "The Joneses"? Are you living your life based on your true wants and needs or are your decisions based on what someone else is doing or what society is telling you is acceptable and or expected? Take time to explore what your family's values are and what is truly important. Then be authentic regardless of what society says is "right".

8. Do you spend quality time with your family and friends? Spending quality time with loved ones means being 100% present. Are hectic schedules getting in the way? Is technology getting in the way? Remember that you set an example for those around you. If you are always on your phone and checking to see if something is more important than the person(s) that you are currently spending time with, then the message is clearly received and the behavior is quickly learned.

Does any of this strike a chord? Recognizing activities, commitments and the choices we make each day is the first step to establishing balance. It is time to embrace our perfectly imperfect lives and let go of the expectation of perfection. It is time to start devoting our energy to what is most important and be realistic about what we want to manage. It is time to get off the wheel.

We will help you get there.

III. THE PAUSE

Be careful of your thoughts, for your thoughts become your words.
Be careful of your words, for your words become your actions.
Be careful of your actions, for your actions become your habits.
Be careful of your habits, for your habits become your character.
Be careful of your character, for your character becomes your destiny.
— Chinese proverb, author unknown

W hen we first started in this business, we had clients who continually called us in to tidy up the same mayhem over and over again. Though repeat business is nice, we wanted to help them change their habits so that our services would no longer be needed. We began to take note of the thought and behavior patterns that seemed to be preventing the life of simplicity our clients were imagining. It did not take us long to realize that with some coaching from us, along with effort and practice on the part of our clients, poor habits could change permanently. This lesson taught us that cultivating a balanced life encompasses more than clearing the physical clutter, it also involves clearing mental clutter. So, before we start conquering the cabinets packed with Tupperware and drawers jammed with paperwork, we must first focus on the inside.

The role we play in governing our lives can get lost in the hurry and stress of our circumstances. If we slowed down and took a moment to think through a given situation, would we take a different approach? A moment before we ask a question, answer a question, make an accusation, send an email or a text. A moment before we stack our mail on the counter and walk away, leave clothes in the laundry basket to deal with later, or spend money on things we do not need.

Our thoughts, words and actions do not need to be spontaneous. They have a beginning, steadily rising up like waves. During this time, we have the ability to let the seeds (our thoughts) take root and manifest into words and/ or actions, or to change course and allow them to subside. This practice requires us to be completely present. A watcher of our minds. So how do we accomplish this? By learning to pause.

A few years ago, we witnessed tension between a husband and wife regarding the need for our services. This is also when we discovered the absolute necessity of the pause. Words were flying out of Bill's mouth before he even knew what he had said. We overlooked the jabs at his wife and his constant huffing and puffing. We worked around the space he occupied and around the numerous piles spread about the kitchen counter and table. His behavior angered Jane, and she responded with curt comments back.

This called for a meeting at Vintage, one of our favorite local coffee houses, to discuss and analyze the situation so that we could comfortably move forward with the project. The more we talked, the more we gained insight into the importance of the pause.

As we worked with Jane, we began to enforce the value of pausing in all aspects of the project, including how to communicate her need for a simpler life to her husband. Eventually Bill came around, somewhat, when he witnessed a transformation in Jane's work, sleep habits and overall spirit. He was reaping the benefits and whether he admitted it or not, he was enjoying a new peace in their relationship. Gradually he got on board, learned to hold his tongue and let us tackle the chaotic state of his paperwork.

The Pause is the space between a thought and a response or action.

Learning to pause and be mindful before we act will allow us to recognize our habits and patterns of our behavior. Once we uncover why we behave as we do, we are better able to open ourselves up to transformation.

Here are some things to ponder as you discover the pause:

1. Am I doing what is easy or what is right? Taking short cuts will cheat us out of the experience and set a bad example to those around us who are learning from our actions.

2. Am I willing to pay the price for my actions? If we pause and take a moment to think through a situation, we may prevent hurt feelings and/or harmful choices.

3. Do I want it or do I need it? If we wait at least 24 hours before purchasing an item, we may discover that we really do not want or need it after all - and look at the money saved!

4. Are distractions affecting my choices/actions? Are powerful tools like social media, Internet and cell phones dominating our lives and, without proper boundaries, resulting in the loss of valuable time? Do the extra responsibilities you have taken on affect quality time spent with family? The distractions from the constant bombardment of mental clutter affects our health and overall well-being making living in the present virtually impossible. Stop, take time to pause, and think about where your time is best served.

We all know that our minds are like monkeys, jumping from one thing to the next with little notice. One minute we are thinking about what to make for dinner and the next we are on to how desperately we need a pedicure. With this said, we might feel it is impossible to slow down and learn to pause. Breaking habits or routines that have been in place for years is possible with practice, but we must be patient and diligent. The more we pause, the easier it becomes. The benefits are clear: reduced stress, anxiety and mental clutter. It is a practice, there is no doubt about it, but one with instant results. And isn't that what we are all after?

Our objective is to encourage our clients to become mindful of their thoughts and behavior. To slow down and allow for time to disconnect from the world and breathe. Only then can we become more realistic about what we can and want to manage. The results are life changing!

There are many techniques we can use to quiet our minds – prayer, meditation, yoga and journaling are some of the most effective. Once you have found a method that feels natural to you, stick with it. Consistency and practice are key. With time, you will discover that your ability to pause, choose words and actions wisely, and think clearly will be more prevalent. Not only will you notice the change, your loved ones will as well (see RESOURCES in the back of the book for techniques).

Start right now. Focus on the present. Each day is a blank canvas. Practice the pause. It is time to invite peace, calm and function in and set chaos free. When we learn to think differently, we can then live differently!

Now, with calm minds, we can move on to the physical clutter.

IV. THE ART OF LETTING GO
The Four Simple Nest Questions

All the art of living lies in a fine mingling of letting go and holding on.
-Havelock Ellis

T he home is the foundation from which everything spills and should be a place that is both nurturing and calm. When we live in excess, we no longer have the physical or spiritual space necessary to achieve our potential. Holding on to excess can increase anxiety, stress, and risk for falls.

Step back and take inventory of all you have to manage. Is it depleting you of precious time, energy and money? The things we hold on to can have a dangerous grip on us. We may love an object or, we may just be keeping it because it reminds us of a special person, place or thing. What is important to remember, whether we love the object or not, is that it does not have a soul or feelings.

It should serve a purpose. Whether that purpose is to celebrate us or a loved one, or provide a useful service, it is still just an object.

We recognize the value of treasuring the past and planning for the future, but our goal should be to surround ourselves with what we love, what inspires us and what is functional and useful in our present-day life. Not every item in our home will be difficult to let go of but realize the process cannot be done in one weekend. As you begin to purge, you will find yourself experiencing a wonderful trek down memory lane. This is a time to be enjoyed and treasured and a time to appreciate your past while contributing to someone else's future.

We had an amazing "aha moment" years back when working with our lovely client Anne. She had lived in her historic downtown Charleston home for over 30 years and had raised her family there. The time had come to downsize, and she was moving into a townhouse just around the corner. Anne was feeling overwhelmed as her house was only days away from being placed on the market and time was of the essence. We were hired to coordinate the move and help her pare down to only the items that would go to her new home. Most importantly, we would help Anne maintain her sanity during the process.

Anne's beautiful two-story home had an attic and basement bursting with history and treasures. She had lived through the Great Depression and we were able to recognize that letting go of personal possessions would prove difficult for her. Though the project would have to be done quickly, we would not let her feel rushed. Ultimately, we took turns working with Anne and we both found her to be witty and full of charm. So, while one of us would run around the house dealing with donation trucks, movers and 1-800-Got-Junk, the other would patiently sit with Anne going through box after box of treasured memories and items.

On the first morning of the project, we pulled boxes down from the attic that had been labeled "Fine Linens". We decided to begin the work together so that we could get an idea of how Anne would react to the process and whether or not we would need to implement a new strategy. Kneeling before her as she sat on the bed, we held up each yellowed napkin, placemat and delicate, hand stitched handkerchief for her to view. It became clear that Anne had the need to touch each piece and tell us its history before she could let it go. It was her way of saying good-bye. We helped her realize that the memory had been within her all along, not in the object. This enabled her to decipher what she truly loved and wanted to keep versus what she was holding onto for memory's sake. The process became easier for her as we went through china, crystal, pictures and other treasures and we could see the weight being lifted from her right before our eyes. Learning to let go of objects, that have once meant so much, is a true art and by the time we moved Anne into her new home, she had mastered it.

Working with Anne allowed us to discover a new level of patience and reminded us of how tailored each project needs to be. More importantly, we learned that we are merely guides on someone else's journey, and this lesson would help us tremendously in our work going forward.

The Four Simple Nest Questions

In our tenure in this business, we can tell right away

what items inspire our clients as they go through their homes, just as we can tell those items they are torn about keeping, but do not hold dear. Realizing that every situation is unique allowed us to narrow down our list of questions to the following four when helping clients decide what to keep and what to purge. These same questions will help you determine what stays and what can, even reluctantly, go.

1. Do I love it and does it celebrate me? When you see this item does it make you happy? Does it celebrate who you are and what you are passionate about? The possessions that we surround ourselves with should make us smile and/ or celebrate our style. When you set up your space, let it be defined by your personality and interests. Show off your adventures and what's most sentimental. Leave spaces empty until you have just the right treasure to place in it. Avoid what we call "fillers" – an item purchased for the sake of filling a space that has no connection to you.

2. Is it useful and functional on a regular basis (or have I worn it in the last year?) Yes, a bread maker is useful and functional but not if it has been collecting dust for five years! Holding on to an item because you may use it or need it one day, or because "sometimes I use it for…" is usually pointless. Do we really need a platter just for asparagus or a basket just for hamburger buns? Probably not. In our business, it is called the "What if?" question and the one we hear the most. You will no doubt be faced with this question as you begin to simplify, and it's a question that can set you back if you let it. If the day ever comes that you need the item, chances are, you have something else that fits the bill or you can borrow it.

3. Can it serve another purpose in my home? If you love the item but have not been utilizing it, can it take on a new responsibility in your home? Perhaps old teacups and crystal bowls can corral jewelry and make-up or hold paperclips in your desk drawer. Baskets and vintage boxes can store ribbons, scarves and belts; large and small crocks can house kitchen utensils, umbrellas and wrapping paper; jars can hold cereal and snacks (and you can see when you are running low). If you love it, you can find a use for it!

As you begin to clear the excess, keep an eye out for

items that can be used for storage. Baskets, jars, trays and large bowls can replace the need to purchase plastic bins, making for unique, money saving storage. Think outside of the box, get creative and be mindful of the environment.

4. Would I buy it again if I had the opportunity? Would you really? This is the question that ends up being the most difficult for our clients to stomach. You will ask yourself many times over "Why did I ever buy this?". Though it can be a bit painful, it is also eye opening. The money we spontaneously spend on stuff, without thinking through our purchases, can be costly. Buying an item in haste usually ends up being wasteful. You will find that those items will be the first to go.

Working toward a life of simplicity can mean something different to each of us and we are all on our own journey. Be patient as you go through the rooms in your home and be sure to use The Four Simple Nest Questions. With some items, you may decide after one question and with other items, you will ask all four. We promise the process will get easier and easier!

V. CAST ASIDE WITH CARE

*The earth will not continue to offer its harvest, except with faithful
stewardship. We cannot say we love the land and then take steps to
destroy it for use by future generations.*
- Pope John Paul II

Hollywood, SC, is a rural town located about 20 miles from Charleston. We would be clearing the house of Jan and Benjamin, an older couple who moved to a retirement community. Our contact would be their daughter, Cecelia, who lived in another state. We knew immediately that this project was going to be a doozy when we pulled up to the house for the first time. This would be the project where we would use all of our resources for proper disposal and donation.

As we worked our way through the house, it became evident that, because of the couple's deteriorating health, things had just been let go. But as we sorted through their personal possessions, it was clear that at one time this couple had been very energetic about life and the world they lived in. There were tons of photographs documenting their travels, books on every subject you could think of, and banners and protest signs depicting their political views. They were intelligent and passionate, and we knew we would have liked them very much if we had met them.

We always come away from a job with a couple of memorable experiences, and this job would be no exception. One early morning, while boxing up the hundreds of books for donation to the library, we heard a strange scraping sound coming from the outside of the house. Twice, we bravely opened the front door and peered out to find nothing there. The noise continued, and, with phones and a baseball bat in hand, we descended the front porch steps, shoulder-to-shoulder, and called out to see if anyone would answer. Silence. After taking a quick peek around the yard, we picked up the pace and headed back toward the front door only to freeze when the noise broke out again. We both looked up at the same time to witness seven of the largest vultures we have ever seen on top of the roof lined up like soldiers reporting for duty. Screaming and running at a pace neither of us knew we had, we made it inside the house and slammed and locked the door – to make sure the birds couldn't break in.

The next day, more drama as we opened a Christmas box that had been stored in the attic, only to find two dead mice lying amongst a nativity scene. The day after that we would find ourselves running for cover when opening a kitchen cabinet that displayed a note saying, "Some of these canned goods have exploded and may contain botulism." None of the cans had been removed.

The days following, while working in the basement and garage, we encountered mold and an abundance of chemicals, oils and cleaners that needed to be properly recycled and disposed of. (If we'd had HAZMAT suits, we would have worn them!) We opened a box that contained the skcletal remains of what looked like a dog and right after, encountered a snake coiled up in the corner of the garage from which our screams could be heard two counties over! After getting the situation under control, we called recycling centers to see which ones accepted what, and carefully transported the above (minus the skeletal remains and the snake), along with an abundance of small non-working appliances, cords and electronics, to the appropriate facilities.

Needless to say, this job wore us completely out. We had visited several recycling centers, dropped off donations to our favorite organizations, donated a massive number of books to the local library and to one of our favorite local book stores Blue Bicycle Books, and coordinated local vendors to meet us at the house to purchase items that would bring income to Jan and Benjamin. Most importantly, we were able to assure Cecelia that the contents of the house had been properly donated and safely disposed of.

If you are ready to begin clearing the clutter, focus on one area at a time. Start small, with the least sentimental items in your home, even a junk drawer, and work your way up to the bigger spaces. This will give you a sense of accomplishment and prepare you for the bigger decisions.

Tips:

1. Always be mindful of The Four Simple Nest Questions:

- Do I LOVE it and does it celebrate me?

- Is it useful and functional on a regular basis

(or have I worn it in the last year)?

• Can it serve another purpose in my home?

• Would I buy it again if I had the opportunity?

2. Set up four boxes or bags and label:

    • Donate

    • Sell

    • Recycle

    • Trash

Note: Avoid using plastic bags if possible, especially for recyclables.

If it's time to let go of the item, here are some great options:

1. Sell your item. There are several options when thinking of selling but keep in mind, like a car driven off the lot, the item will not have the value it had before it was taken out of the store. Take a picture of the item(s) and do one of the following: Use a safe social network site to market it for sale, visit a local antique market to inquire about dealer interest, or contact a local consignment shop to see interest in selling for you, splitting the profit.

2. Donate your item. When you donate an item, you are bringing relief, comfort and pleasure to others. There are many organizations in the community that can benefit from your outreach. Research programs in your area that pull at your heartstrings. It's a great way to serve others and it will make you feel good. If you find that you have an abundance to donate, there are charitable organizations that will pick up your donations at your home (see RESOURCES in the back of the book for a list of some of our favorite organizations).

3. Recycle your item. Make sure and take the time to dispose of unwanted items properly. Not all recycling centers will accept electronics, mattresses and paint. Learn where your recycling centers are and what they will accept.

As you cast aside those items in your home that are no longer relevant to you, be aware of organizations that can benefit from your extras. Keep our Earth in mind when determining what is trash and what can be recycled. Not only will you be setting a good example for the next generation, but you will be helping to leave the next generation with a healthier place to live.

VI. HEIRLOOMS AND THE FINER THINGS

Our most treasured family heirloom are our sweet family memories.
The past is never dead, it is not even past.
-William Faulkner

Living in historic Charleston, South Carolina has played an immense role in shaping our business. Many of our projects involve homes packed with family heirlooms and treasures of historical significance. These homes, like all homes, must be treated with kind and careful hands. Understanding the provenance of our discoveries has been a journey with a tremendous learning curve. With that said, we would agree that the most valuable thing we have learned is not how much objects are worth, but the importance of using what you love every day.

Recently, while sipping lattes at Second State Coffee and finalizing the details for our next project, a young woman sat down next to us and pulled from a pouch a carefully wrapped teacup and saucer. Curious, we watched her as she unveiled her treasured pieces. She then ordered hot tea and handed the server her cup and saucer. Our mouths dropped, she was a girl after our own hearts! We introduced ourselves and asked about her teacup. She told us that she loves the ritual of drinking out of her favorite collection of cups and celebrating the treasures in her life. "Life is fragile," she said "but you don't stop living. Use what you love, even if it is delicate, and don't hide it away. Plus, I feel like I am helping to preserve our environment and protect our planet." This epitomizes our philosophy!

We have found gorgeous, pricy and sentimental pieces buried in drawers, closets, attics and garages. Many of these pieces are family heirlooms and have been hidden away and forgotten, failing to celebrate the memory of the person who once owned them. Why not create new memories and begin using these pieces, no matter how fragile? For example, most all of our clients have valuable pieces of sterling silver tucked away and rarely, if ever, use them. Silver flatware is notorious for camping out in dining room drawers anxiously awaiting the opportunity to shine at the next dinner party. Sadly, for most, glorious dinner parties are always just a daydream away, happening once or twice a year – at best. When we present the idea of moving the silver to the kitchen drawer for daily use, the normal reaction is a look of horror. But we guarantee that if you pull out your most beautiful things, and use them, it will make you feel good. After all, isn't everyday deserving of your best?

Some of our more mature clients, who decide the time has come to downsize, own fabulous antique pieces such as chests of drawers, high boys, gilded mirrors, and more, tell us that their children have expressed no interest in receiving these beautiful items - they want new and modern, none of the "brown stuff". We have learned that one of the best, foolproof design tips is to mix old and new to make your home interesting and unique. Owning a piece of history that tells a story about your family has a value all of its own. Thankfully, we have been able to encourage and show some of the next generation how to make these pieces work in their homes, much to their surprise.

Heirlooms can be repurposed. Silver trays can be separated from a tea set to make a statement on a coffee table. Antique bowls can be used instead of box store finds to corral jewelry and make-up. We can discover our creative side by refinishing or painting old pieces - some may just need a coat of polish and some TLC. It is easy to breathe new life into a piece just by changing the knobs and topping it with more modern items like pictures with cool frames, a modern vase with flowers, stacked books we love, etc. And, when we give new life and purpose to older items, it is gentle on the earth and our wallet (see RESOURCES in the back of the book for quick tips on repurposing).

As we go through the process, heirlooms and those finer pieces will need to be dealt with. We understand that they are not as easy as going through clothes, coffee mugs or beach towels. The attachment we have for items that once belonged to loved ones makes them especially hard to part with. So, what is the best approach for handling family heirlooms that we can't seem to let go of?

Ask yourself these questions:

1. Are you holding onto the item because you love it?
If you do not love the item or it does not serve a function, donate it or consign it.

2. Are you holding onto the item because you feel guilty getting rid of it? It may bring someone else the pleasure it was intended to give.

3. Does the item really celebrate who that person is or was?
Remember your memories are the most valuable connection to loved ones.

4. Would the original owner want you to be burdened by the item? Was that their intention when passing it to you?

5. Are you keeping the item because it is worth money?
Why not consign or sell the item and use the money to do something you love?

Think about the following before you pass something down or gift an item to a loved one or friend (This is relevant for the giver and the receiver.):

1. Are you contributing to the chaos/clutter in their lives? With clarity recognize if they have enough.

2. Is your goal to eliminate the guilt of giving it away by passing it along to someone else? Many people feel they can escape guilt by passing it on to another member of the family. They feel that as long as it stays in the family it is ok.

3. Don't pass your burdens on to others unless they really love and desire the item. The best way to determine what to give your loved ones is to ask them this open-ended question: "Is there anything from my home that you would like me to hold on to for you?" Let them offer up what their favorite treasures are, you might be surprised. Put the ball in their court.

4. Be willing to hear the word no and don't make them feel guilty about it. The last thing you want is for STUFF to result in a relationship strain.

Go through your home, being completely honest with yourself, and let go of those things that do not meet the criteria of items to keep. You may uncover treasures that have been in hiding for years! Think about how you can switch things up. Move furniture around to serve a different purpose. Be creative! Dealing with heirlooms and the pricier items in your home is a unique process and now you are equipped to handle the challenge.

VII. ROOM BY ROOM

*The greatest step towards a life of simplicity
is to learn to let go.
-Steve Maraboli*

Setting up the spaces in our home to function at their best is key to living simply, and especially important if our spaces are small. We have outlined a process that will get your home in ultimate working order while helping you deal with those projects that give us the greatest amount of agony. You are working on yourself as you go through each room and tackling each project – focus on the inside as you address the outside.

Remember to take your time as you maneuver through rooms and projects. Do not bite off more than you can chew. Savor your sense of accomplishment and let that be your motivation to continue. Most importantly, begin each project with the intention of completing it in a proper timeframe!

THE COMMAND CENTER ─────────

Many of us find ourselves frantically looking for a bill, a tax record, that permission slip for our child and more because we have formed the habit of stacking. We have stacks all over the house for things "to get to later". For any home to run smoothly, it is critical for paperwork, receipts and bills to be in order and easily accessible. We call this our command center and it keeps us on top of our game. No desk? No worries! You can find nice file boxes at local office supply stores that can easily be stored and pulled out when needed. We discovered a vintage file drawer on wheels at a local antique store for one of our clients that met her needs perfectly. When not in use, she uses it as side table. Be creative!

Tips:

1. Create four bins, boxes or bags labeled:

- Keep

- Recycle

- Shred

- Trash

2. Walk around your entire home and gather all paperwork and mail stacked on counters and stuffed in drawers and begin to separate into the categories above.

3. Set aside your keep pile for file preparation and dispose of the other piles properly.

4. If you do not own a shredder, you can take documents to an office supply store and pay to shred by the pound or bring them to a free-shred event.

5. Set up files. A good filing system is key for success. We have outlined some of the more important files that you should create, but lifestyles and situations vary so you may

need more or less. At least quarterly, properly discard papers no longer needed. With access to many of your statements and other documents online, you can create the bare minimum in files. But for the files you do make, use a label maker or black sharpie in clear and neat handwriting. Why? Because neatness inspires organization.

Recommended File Labels:

Bills To Be Paid - A file for bills to be paid is crucial. Not only will this keep incoming bills organized but they will be close at hand. Keep this file in front for easy access.

Bills Paid - For bills that you want to keep for your records, separate by month and paperclip, then label the month and year on the front.

Medical Bills Paid/Health Insurance Claims - Keep track of what your insurance covers. Any time your insurance company sends an EOB form with the breakdown of what has been covered, review and compare to your medical bill, staple together and then file. Highlight the name of the family member service was for. Even insurance companies make mistakes and you want to keep track of your deductible paid! Most insurance companies have the Explanation of Benefit statement online now. You can print out, or create an online file to include a scanned copy of your medical bill. Either way, it is crucial that you create the system that works best for you.

Health Care Provider - Information regarding what your health insurance covers is nice to have on hand when big decisions need to be made regarding personal health for your family.

Individual Family Members - Files for copies of important papers such as social security cards, birth certificates, vaccination records and other important personal information. Read on to see where to house the originals.

School - Having additional files for each family member are preferred because by the end of the year these files can really fill up. Group all files together.

Pets - File medical records and other information.

Automobiles - Repair and maintenance documents. You can also keep these together in the glove compartment of your car.

Utility Providers - Security, cable, cell phone provider, pest, etc.

Home Repairs And Improvements - Maintaining accurate and well-kept records are important for you and for the re-sale of your home.

Tax File For The Current Year - Collect receipts and all other tax records needed to complete your income taxes. This is super important and will make life much easier when time to file!

Note: We recommend a separate file box for home manuals and instruction booklets as they can take up a lot of room and very seldom need to be pulled out.

In addition to, or in lieu of, a safe deposit box, purchase a home safe to house important paperwork that is difficult to replace. For each member of the family, label the front of a large manila envelope to house original birth certificate, social security card, passport, etc. For other important paperwork, create nicely labeled files. If original items are not kept in a bank safe deposit box, keep them here. It is also important to have an extra copy of each safely stored in another location.

Recommended items for home safe or bank safe deposit box:
- Social security cards
- Passports
- Birth certificates, death certificates
- Court Documents - Wills, Marriage Certificate, Divorce Decree, etc.
- Notes Paid
- Home Owner's/Flood Insurance Declaration Pages
- Life Insurance Policies
- Other financial documents you deem private and/or important that may be time consuming to replace.

From now on, when you get the mail, touch it once. This will prevent you from becoming overwhelmed by bills and paperwork. Go through your mail over the recycle bin and eliminate what you do not need. File any bills and items to keep right away. It is also good idea to update your calendar with due dates as you go through mail.

Note: See RESOURCES in the back of the book for Earth friendly tips to reduce your mail and what important documents you need to keep, and for how long.

CLOSETS

It is refreshing to start each season with an organized and functional closet. As seasons change, it's important to look through your closets and drawers and pull out items you did not wear, no longer like or that no longer serve a purpose in your life. It is a fact that we wear 25% of our clothes 75% of the time! So, a lot of clothes just sit and collect dust. Time to clear it out!

Tips:

1. Have four large bags marked:

- Donate

- Recycle

- Sell

- Trash

2. Research the consignment stores in your area. This is a great way to earn some extra cash for clothes in good condition. Make sure to call ahead to see if they are accepting clothes for a particular season and what their rules are.

3. Local websites for selling items online are also a great way to sell clothes and other merchandise. Once you join you just take a picture of your items, post and get paid! And there are no cutbacks to a third party.

4. Clear all the empty hangers out of your closet and put in a pile.

5. Remove items that do not belong in your closet and put them where they do belong.

6. Start with small sections at a time instead of pulling everything out of your closet at once. By starting small, you are less likely to become overwhelmed and you can stop when you get tired, or have something else to tend to, without leaving a big mess.

7. Begin with a category, i.e. tops and blouses. Go through your closet pulling out all that apply to that category. Make sure you check pockets as you pull clothes out.

8. With each article of clothing and accessory in your closet ask yourself The Four Simple Nest Questions:

> • Do I LOVE it and does it celebrate me?
>
> • Is it useful and functional on a regular basis (or have I worn it in the last year)?
>
> • Can it serve another purpose in my home?
>
> • Would I buy it again if I had the opportunity?

9. Examine clothing and accessories and discard if time has taken its toll. And definitely discard, donate or sell if it no longer fits, is uncomfortable or is not your authentic style.

10. If you are still unsure, hang the item back in your closet with the hanger facing the opposite way. After you wear the item put the hanger back the correct way. If after the appropriate season the hanger is still backwards and you did not wear it, get rid of it!

11. Take the time to wipe down your shelves and vacuum before putting clothes back in.

THE LINEN CLOSET———————————

The linen closet clean-out is always so refreshing. Being able to open the door of the closet and see nicely folded linens and towels is beyond satisfying!

Tips:

1. Pull out all sheets and donate or discard those that no longer fit the beds in your home and/or are worn and have holes and

tears. Be reasonable about how many sets of sheets you actually need. Two sets are a good rule of thumb.

2. Now that you have pared down, look online at a YouTube video that shows you how to fold sheets properly so that they line up and look nice in your linen closet.

3. Pull out all of your towels and examine their condition. If they need to be replaced, and your budget allows, now is a good time to do so. Again, consider the number you actually need and then fold towels neatly.

4. Before returning any linens and towels to your closet, make sure and wipe down shelves with a green cleaner. We like to keep a nice bottle of linen spray in the closet to keep every-thing smelling fresh until their next use.

Note: Old towels can be donated to animal shelters in your community to keep furry friends warm.

PANTRY ————————————————

Starting your clean-out in the pantry before tackling the kitchen will be easier and get you motivated to continue on to the kitchen (which will most likely be one of the biggest projects in your home).

The pantry should be cleaned out at least once a month to determine what you need, what has expired and what you can donate to a local food bank. Be mindful of all the processed foods you are buying as you begin to clean out and consider healthier options for your family. From here on out, keep pantry shelves uncluttered so that all items are visible and not forgotten.

Tips:

1. Pull out any stale or expired food and compost if possible (see RESOURCES in the back of the book for composting information).

2. Box up items that can be donated to the local food bank. Check expiration dates.

3. Wipe down cabinet doors or pantry door and shelves with green cleaner.

4. Wipe off oil, vinegars and honey bottles and jars.

5. Keep like items together and place items used the most at eye level.

6. Invest in clear jars to place crackers, cereals, pastas and grains in. This allows you to see when an item is running low - and they look pretty on the shelf.

7. Repurpose baskets and vintage boxes to corral snacks and other goods. This looks nice and allows items to be seen, eliminating more boxes.

Note: See RESOURCES in the back of the book for tips on preventing food waste.

KITCHEN ─────────────────────

The kitchen is the heart of the home. Family and friends

gravitate to this room where conversation is warm and appetites are satisfied. It does not matter if your kitchen is large or small, it is about utilizing your space efficiently and minimizing excess. With a little creativity and patience, you can set up a kitchen that functions well and inspires you to cook. By setting up stations to create a smooth work flow, your kitchen can function and perform at its best. Believe us when we say, this could take several rearrangements! We are sharing some ideas that have worked for us, and for our clients, so take a peek and tailor your kitchen stations to meet your needs. The time you invest in this project is definitely worth it and you will find that your heart of the home is exactly where you want everyone to be.

Tips:

1. Have a donation box ready.

2. Start with one drawer or cabinet at a time and pull everything out.

3. Use a counter top and/or tabletop to sort like items, i.e.: cooking tools, serving utensils, storage items, serving trays, etc.

4. Ask yourself The Four Simple Nest Questions:

> • Do I LOVE it and does it celebrate me?
>
> • Is it useful and functional on a regular basis (or have I worn it in the last year)?
>
> • Can it serve another purpose in my home?
>
> • Would I buy it again if I had the opportunity?

5. Donate those items that you have not used or have duplicates of. We know that in some cases you do need duplicates but be realistic. Unless you are a caterer no one needs ten 13x9 Pyrex pans.

6. Clean each space with green cleaner before placing items you are keeping back in.

7. Place kitchen tools in vintage crocks or other treasured pieces and keep on the counter for easy access when cooking.

8. Place pots and pans convenient to the stove for easy access.

9. Organize plates and glasses near the dishwasher making unloading easier.

10. Set up coffee, tea, cups and saucers near your coffee pot or electric teakettle.

11. Group all baking supplies together and place close to where you do your baking. Pour flours and sugars in glass jars and label.

12. Go through your spices and make sure none have expired and store all of your spices near the stove where you use them most. However, make sure they are not in an area that will get over-heated (like above the stove) as it shortens the lifespan of the spice.

13. Do not keep every appliance you own on the counter as this reduces your workspace. Appliances that you use less frequently can be placed in the cabinet below or above for

easy access. If space is an issue for storing appliances, ask yourself if you really need it or if another tool in your kitchen can serve the same purpose.

14. Place large pots, crock pots and other items used less frequently in less accessible places like above the stove, refrigerator or highest cabinet.

15. Create a prep area. Think about how you use your kitchen and where you stand to bake, make lunches, and prep dinner. Then set up your work area to be efficient so that you are not going back and forth within the kitchen.

16. Hang pots if possible. This creates extra room in the drawers and cabinets.

17. Utilize wall space with magnetic strips for knives and spices. Take advantage of the end of your counters or islands by hanging hooks or a towel bar with "S" hooks to hang long kitchen utensils that do not fit in a drawer.

18. Keep kitchen towels near the sink and hot pads near the oven for quick access.

19. Use Lazy Susans in your cabinets, pantry and refrigerator for quick access to items.

20. Find a convenient spot for recipe books that you love and donate those that you never use. Each time you try a new recipe, note on the page if it was a success or failure. We use smiley and frowney faces.

LAUNDRY ROOM ————————————————

Keeping up with the laundry in your home can be a daunting task. And, if you have a full house, it becomes more difficult. But even with this task, we can maintain control with some simple steps:

Tips:

1. Use your space wisely, many laundry rooms are the size of a small closet. Be creative and mount a shelf to the wall and hooks to the back of the door if needed. The back of the

door is also a great place to hang your ironing board. Adding a countertop to the tops of your washer and dryer creates a great work space for sorting and folding if your washer is a front loader.

2. Organize products and supplies according to how they are used. Items used regularly should be within easy reach; corral extra supplies and incidentals and place in an out of the way spot.

3. Keep a bin in the laundry room or mud room for icky stuff you do not want in the hamper - like dirty soccer clothes and kitchen rags. Galvanized tubs work great placed on top of the dryer. Add a cute label.

4. Label your laundry bins for dirty clothes i.e. darks, lights, and delicates for easier sorting at wash time. Luggage tags work great for this.

5. To keep the hamper from getting "stinky", add a few drops of essential oils to a washcloth and place it in the bottom of the hamper.

6. Use lingerie bags to keep small items together like socks and underwear.

7. Have a drying rack handy for items to drip-dry. This is also a great way to preserve clothes and save energy.

8. If you have a front load washer, wipe away any moisture from the inside opening and door of washer to prevent mold and mildew. Be sure to clean out the dryer lint tray after each dry cycle to prevent a fire hazard. At least once a week, use a damp cloth to wipe down the top of machines.

9. Make it a rule that all dirty clothes must make it into the hamper each day.

10. Assign a small laundry basket to each family member and attach a tag with their name neatly printed on it. As you fold your clean laundry, sort each item into the assigned basket. Better yet, have each family member fold his or her own laundry!

11. Each family member should be responsible for picking up their basket and putting away their clean clothing.

12. Help little ones be independent by putting pictures of clothing items on their drawers so they know where to put their clean clothes.

13. This might be a bit cruel, but don't do any more laundry until family members put away their clothes! You will be amazed at how well this works.

14. Keep single socks together that always seem to lose their mate. Find a jar or bin and label it "Looking for a Mate".

BATHROOM

The bathroom can become a catchall for everything from household cleaners to extra toilet paper and sundries. Paring down to just the essentials reduces chaos and allows room for storage.

Tips:

1. If you store cleaning products in your bathroom, begin using just one or two green cleaners. A good All-Purpose Cleaner should do the trick if you are consistent with keeping your bathroom clean.

2. If you prefer not to use a toilet brush holder that lives by the toilet, find a small trash can that can be easily cleaned to house your brush, and store with your other cleaning products under the sink (if you have cabinets). Be sure to clean the toilet bowl brush after each use, the same rule applies to your plunger!

3. If you have open storage versus bathroom cabinets, find trays, pretty baskets or neat crates to coral cosmetics, toilet paper, hair tools, towels, etc. Always storing like items together.

4. Use pretty bowls or tea cups that you already have on hand (or shop your local antique markets and thrift shops) to corral hair accessories, make-up and nail products.

5. For more storage, install additional towel hooks or bars. Add wall shelves, or a medicine cabinet, for make-up and sundries.

Note to bulk shoppers: Keeping a specified space for your extra supplies will keep things neat and allow you to easily check quantities before your next big bulk shopping trip. Be careful though, an oversupply of basic essentials can be somewhat stressful if you have limited space. Sometimes, bulk shoppers tend to buy the same items with each trip before they have made a dent in what they already have. It can be a very expensive habit when the original intention was to save money.

COSMETICS

Chances are that over the last year or so you have accumulated numerous "miracle" products you have not used. With the constant bombardment of advertisements, we are sucked into purchasing cosmetics that end up collecting dust. In addition, we hold on to favorites way past their expiration dates, trying to get every last drop out of the bottle. Time to clear out!

Tips:

1. Get rid of all expired products. Below are some guidelines for what needs to go and when.

- Eyeliner: 6 months to 1 yr.

- Mascara: 3-6 months

- Blush, eye shadow & other powder cosmetics: 1-2 yrs.

- Foundation: 6 months to 2 yrs.

- Lipstick: 2 yrs.

- Natural products: 3-6 months

2. Throw out or give away anything you do not use. Be completely honest with yourself and do not be swayed by how much you paid for it. Let it go if you do not use it.

3. Wipe down area with a green cleaner.

4. Pull out a few pretty treasures to store your makeup, creams and potions in. Tea cups you love but never use, little silver trays and crystal bowls are great storage.

5. Moving forward, think twice before purchasing items

you rarely use. Even if you love the idea of a toner, do not purchase it unless you plan on making it part of your routine.

MEDICINES & FIRST AID ————————————

As you conquer the bathroom it is essential to clean out the medicine cabinet as well. Disposing of outdated medicines properly is not only a safety issue, but an environmental issue as well. Scientists have learned that medications thrown in the garbage can actually get into our soil creating an environmental hazard. Flushing expired medicines seems to be the safest way of disposal because there is no danger of children and pets accidentally ingesting pills. However, studies have shown that this option presents an environmental hazard as well because small traces of certain medications have actually showed up in our water supplies.

So, what to do? Many pharmacies and police stations now offer drug recycling programs. Some will take your medications back anytime and make sure they are disposed of properly, while others will hold drives to collect your expired meds. Be sure to call around to other local pharmacies if your pharmacy does not participate in some type of recycling program. You can also contact your local hazardous waste facility to get their recommendations on proper disposal. The FDA does have a list of harmful medications on their website that, though safe used as prescribed, are extremely harmful if accidentally ingested by someone else in your household. There are some medications that are not accepted in the pharmacy take back program and, therefore, the FDA does recommend that the safest way of disposal is by flushing. To find a list of these meds, visit their website and search disposal of unused medication (see RESOURCES in the back of this book).

Tips:

1. Corral all of the medications/supplements and vitamins in the house.

2. Pull aside medications and supplements that have expired or that you do not use or plan on using. Take medications to your local pharmacy if they participate in a take back program or check the FDA website for proper disposal (see Resources in the back of the book).

3. Store medicines and first aid products properly to protect them from becoming less potent or from going bad before their actual expiration date. Ask your local pharmacist if there are special storage instructions for your specific medications.

4. Store medications and first aid out of sight and reach of children. If possible, store in a cabinet with a childproof lock. (First aid needs to be easily accessible for you in case of emergencies.)

5. Store medications in a cool and dry place away from heat, moisture, air and light which will cause damage.

6. Do not store medication near your kitchen stove, oven, sink or refrigerator.

7. Do not store medication in a small bathroom as heat and moisture from your shower or bath can cause damage.

8. Always take the cotton ball out of the medicine bottle as it pulls moisture into the bottle.

9. Keep medicine in original containers if possible.

10. Keep all medications together in a labeled, air-tight container with lid. This is the rare occasion that we like to use plastic bins because they are easy to wash out should something spill, and they can be stacked to save space. Use individual bins for adult medication, children's medication, vitamins/supplements and first aid. Label the bins accordingly.

Note: See RESOURCES in the back of the book for tips on stocking your first aid bin for home and car.

GARAGE/UTILITY ROOM ──────────────

The garage, along with the basement and attic, tends to be one of the last places in the home we conquer. It is dirtier than the rest of the house and has more surprises, aka critters. So, as you venture into this daunting space do not forget your gloves and possibly a mask to protect yourself from the unknown. If you have a nice sunny day, and plenty of time, it is a great idea to pull everything out of the garage so you can give it a good sweep before you set up stations in the space.

Tips:

1. Utilize The Four Simple Nest Questions as you go through each item in the garage. Be realistic! If you have a lawn service and have not used your mower in 5 years do you really think one day you might?

- Do I LOVE it and does it celebrate me?
- Is it useful and functional on a regular basis (or have I worn it in the last year)?
- Can it serve another purpose in my home?
- Would I buy it again if I had the opportunity?

2. Corral like items together. For example: Set up a potting bench with all of your garden tools and put kids' toys and bikes in one place. Create a work station for tools and use recycled jelly jars and baby food jars to store nails, screws and other small items – labeled of course.

3. Recycle old paints and chemicals responsibly. Research your local recycle center's website to learn what to bring where. Often the recycle centers that accept chemicals and paints are specific and limited. This is a good opportunity to

go green, get rid of toxic fertilizers and insecticides, and go with organic products.

4. Think vertically. Typically garages have plenty of wall space to add hooks, pegboards, and shelves. Storing items off the floor not only frees up space, but also will keep dust and dirt at bay.

5. Repeat. Think of it as part of your spring-cleaning routine especially if you have young kids and their friends pulling stuff in and out of the garage. Without a doubt it will need a touch up from time to time.

THE ATTIC —————————————

Somehow it is inevitable that the attic ends up being a catch all for just about everything. Just like the garage. Holiday decorations, luggage, old toys and baby clothes, hand-me-downs, you name it! Often, we totally forget about what we have up there and, due to lack of appeal, don't feel like hanging out in the attic long enough to sort through and purge. Keep in mind that, at some point, someone will have to deal with it.

Tips:

1. Ask yourself The Four Simple Nest Questions as you go through each item in the attic.

      • Do I LOVE it and does it celebrate me?

      • Is it useful and functional on a regular basis (or have I worn it in the last year)?

      • Can it serve another purpose in my home?

      • Would I buy it again if I had the opportunity?

2. Corral like items together. For example: Holiday Decorations in one area, luggage in another.

3. Sort through boxes and be reasonable when deciding what to keep. If you only use carry-on luggage on the plane you can let go of the XL suitcases. If you no longer use an artificial tree, let it go.

4. Use plastic bins that can be sealed and labeled when storing

items in the attic. Cardboard boxes are not the best option when storing in spaces that are not climate controlled.

5. Be mindful of storing clothing and soft materials in the attic. The heat and humidity can quickly ruin items meant to be in a climate-controlled space.

6. From now on, don't store anything in the attic just because you don't want to deal with it now. Out of sight, out of mind adds up quickly. Just look at your attic!

TECH CLEANSE ———————————

In today's world we are bombarded with emails, texts and cell phone calls. It is completely overwhelming trying to keep up and clean out! For those of us who just cannot find the time to delete messages and unsubscribe to those emails we no longer want, or for that matter, never signed up for, trust us when we say learning to be consistent with a tech cleanse will prevent insanity!

We devote so much time to our technical devices. We know people who actually gave up social media for Lent!

Our advice is to take several hunks of time to clean up your phones and computers. For those who do not have their devices connected through the "Cloud" and have to delete in two places, this may be a bit more time consuming. However, once you clean up and catch up, you will be glad for the time invested. The goal here will be to learn a couple of new habits.

Tips:

1. When you read an email or text, immediately deal with it. It takes just an extra few seconds really. Here are your choices: Keep, delete, unsubscribe. If you keep it, start the next habit:

2. Set up files on your computer to store emails you need to save. Lifehacker has great tips on how to back up your emails for future use.

3. You can also archive emails on your phone. On most phones, this can be done through your Edit option.

4. It seems the art of conversation is coming in second to connecting with friends and family via email and texts. Think

about letting social media enhance communication within your relationships, not replace it. You may find you have less to delete in your inbox.

VHS TAPES ———————————————————————

In every client's home we come across a stack of VHS tapes without a VHS player anywhere to be found. The tapes hold precious memories of weddings, births and other momentous occasions, yet are virtually obsolete. Unfortunately, these tapes will disintegrate over time and be worthless. Fortunately, they can easily be converted to a DVD or placed on a thumb drive and then stored on a hard drive for back up. A local photography store is a great place to do this conversion. Sometimes they even let you sit down and view the VHS first so you do not spend a chunk of money on a Luau for instance, that lasts 10 hours. There are also mail away companies who will convert your tapes for you.

CHILDREN'S ART AND SCHOOL WORK ——

The more intimate an item, the harder it is to let it go. Children's artwork and handmade creations fall into this category. We would all agree that anything our child makes is special, but should we save every finger-painting?

Tips:

1. Create an art portfolio for each child. This can be a box or bin that slides under the bed of each child.

2. Be consistent and keep only favorites.

3. When you notice the bin getting full, do a quick purge. Pull out a few pieces of art to repurpose as wrapping paper or cut to use as note cards.

BOOKS ────────────────────

We are as guilty as the next with our love of buying new books to read. We love the whole experience of going to the bookstore, browsing to find a good read, drinking a yummy latte, and twenty bucks later leaving with a book that will be finished in a matter of days. Some of us do like to surround ourselves with books by authors we love and that is ok! But, if your books are just stacking up collecting dust and you feel no attachment to your collection, then here are some tips for you.

Tips:

1. Only purchase reference books that you will refer to often.

2. Visit your local library for enjoyment reading. Not only can you save tons of cash and space, but it is also saving trees. Utilizing the library requires planning ahead and reserving books, but with a little patience you can read whatever you like.

3. If the library is not your thing, and you really like holding on to books longer then the due date, Trade-a-Book stores are another great option. De-clutter a few shelves of paperbacks and bring them in for trade. It's a great way to save money and recycle at the same time.

Note: After purging one of our client's bookshelves, they had enough credit to keep them reading for a year!

PICTURES ————————————————

The accumulation of pictures is probably everyone's Achilles heel. Boxes of pictures and albums that we just do not know what to do with! It is the most time consuming and draining of all the projects but also very rewarding. The more personal an item the harder it is to decipher what stays and what goes. That is why we leave this for the end.

Tips:

1. Gather all your pictures and albums in one place.

2. Sort and Purge – Whether you sort by year or event go through every picture and keep your favorites. Do you need 10 pictures of a sunset? Probably not.

3. If you notice photos sticking in old albums pull them out before it is too late. Humidity and adhesives can really do a number on photos over time. They are better off stored in acid-free photo boxes than glued into albums. (If you prefer to store pictures in albums choose albums with acid-free pages, PVC-free sheet protectors or photo corners.)

4. Label dividers by event or year.

5. Store in a climate-controlled part of your home.

6. Scan pictures onto discs or download to USB flash drives.

DIGITAL PICTURES

As mentioned before there is such a thing as digital clutter. With the invention of the smart phone we take pictures of everything from our morning latte to every play of our child's soccer game. All of those photos are stored on our computers, taking up space in a virtual cloud. We have found the best way to deal with the yearly accumulation of digital photos is to create a photo book once a year that documents all of our family's important events and occasions. This can be done online and is a great way to stay on top of your digital life. As you create the book you are forced to go through the years pictures and delete and save as needed. Moving forward you have a treasured collection of books documenting your family's adventures.

ONE FINAL NOTE - Shoes and Feng Shui ———

In Feng Shui tradition, removing our shoes at the door represents leaving worldly goods behind. But there is more to taking off one's shoes then leaving the world behind! Not only will we significantly reduce the amount of dirt tracked into our homes, we also decrease the pesticides, chemicals, and even lead we are exposed to on a daily basis. The U.S Environmental Protection Agency has done studies that show that pesticide-laden shoes are a major source of pesticide exposure, especially in young children who crawl on the floor and put fingers in their mouths. A surprising discovery from these studies also showed that wearing shoes indoors is an even larger source of a child's pesticide exposure than eating non-organic fruits and veggies. So yes, it is Feng Shui but it also keeps the house and body clean! If you have shoes piled up on your porch, in your garage or in a shoe bucket, go through them and get rid of those that are no longer worn.

VIII. DO YOU REALLY NEED MORE SPACE?

Your home is living space, not storage space.
-Francine Jay

We had taken the last flight of stairs to the third floor of the lavish home to see the beginnings of the massive renovation project that would allow each of our client's four children to have their own bedroom and bath. We were hired to help pinpoint where storage would go – after the inevitable purge.

After our tour, we spent the morning on-site brainstorming and taking notes. Then, the two of us reconvened at The Pickled Palate, one of our favorite local cafes, to discuss the ideas we had in mind. This was not an easy task for us because we could think of many great ways to make their current situation work (we would present those ideas as well). Reflecting on the day, and the requests of our client, we could not help but giggle thinking of how our own sons (we each have two) have shared a room for as long as they can remember. We reminisced fondly as we pulled up old photos of our boys on our computers. We agreed that the benefits of sharing a room far outweighed any hardships they had faced. Hopefully they will remember snuggling up and reading bedtime stories and all of the wrestling matches, late-night talks and sleepovers. Without a doubt, they will remember the bitter battles over their lack of space, but they will also remember working it out. The truth is, the memories that our boys have made while bunking up have created a bond that will last a lifetime. We are grateful to know that as our children prepare to leave the nest and go out into the world, sharing space and being patient and accepting of others' differences will hopefully come a little easier to them, as they have spent their whole lives working on it.

Like our clients, many of us have the idea that bigger is better when something small can often times make the biggest difference. The need for more space comes down to the need for more room to breathe. Not only do we want more storage to house our possessions, but we might feel that every child needs their own room, or that every room needs its own purpose. A bigger home is a luxury that is not required for function or happiness. And, more often than not, it is the expense and maintenance of our homes that keeps us from enjoying life's pleasures.

We work with many clients who are ready to renovate or feel the need to move due to a perceived lack of space. In most cases, it is the young client with small children that calls us in to determine the best way to expand their space by adding more cabinets, drawers and closets. In all cases, they are taken aback when we give them the advice of paring down and simplifying before mapping out a renovation blue print. Most heed our advice and in the end, when we have saved them thousands of dollars, are grateful for the life-changing experience.

Before expanding any space, we have to determine why more space is needed. The answer is usually because more excess has been accumulated as the years have passed. However, what we have discovered is that creating more room for storage allows us to accumulate more stuff without discipline. This is why it is important to pay attention to our habits so that we can understand our behavior and begin to make better choices.

The need for more space can also be the result of a growing family. But again, you need to evaluate why more space is needed. For instance, do you want each child to have their own room or does each child indeed need their own room? When siblings learn the fundamentals of being roommates, they develop habits that can better prepare them for life after they leave your nest. Learning to share and respect another's space and needs are difficult lessons that can be effectively learned at an early age.

Rooms in your home can be multifunctional, and for many of us who live small, this is a no brainer. It is how effectively we create these multi-purpose rooms that will allow for a stress free and successful environment. Set up is important, and having the right transition pieces may seem vital, but it is creating the habits and behaviors within your family that are crucial in making any room in your home functional and well kept.

We help our clients get rid of what they no longer

"need" in order to create space to breathe. By eliminating the need for more storage, or at least the original plan for expansion, they are able to rediscover the love they have for their home and better define how it can serve them.

We guarantee that the first step before moving forward with a move or renovation is to completely clear the clutter that is fogging your vision. You will redefine your needs, eliminate an expensive game plan, and celebrate the financial savings enjoyed by living more simply.

IX. STORAGE UNITS

Are you Cheating?

The less you own the less that owns you.
-Grannyism

It was a day of major discovery for us in our business. As we walked through the maze of cold steel and metal trying to find our client's storage unit address, we passed units with open doors where owners were loading or unloading their belongings. We could see furniture, Christmas decorations, bins overloaded with paperwork and even a pinball machine.

We turned left, beginning to feel trapped in this prison of storage cells, and what we saw spread out before us made us stop in our tracks. A couple had just rented a unit and were "moving in". She sat in a fold-up chair talking on her cell phone while he, having set up saw horses, was busy sawing to make the shelves he would be installing to house the chaos that surrounded them.

Apologizing for blocking our way, they quickly felt the need to explain what our jaw-dropping faces were asking. They had cleared their home of all of this "mess" so that they could become more organized. There was something seriously wrong with this picture. They were cheating. Paying for a storage unit to house items no longer needed in our actual home does not simplify our lives but instead, causes financial strain and environmental chaos.

As the need to find additional space to store all of our questionable items increases, our environment suffers. According to Wikipedia, at the time of this book, there are more than 2.35 billion square feet of self-storage in the United States, or a land area equivalent to three times Manhattan Island under roof. Everyday, green space is being cleared to make room for yet another facility to store all of our excess stuff. Next time you drive through your town take notice of all the storage units popping up.

Having frequented these warehouses over the years to help clients, we have never gotten used to the concept of paying for real estate to house stuff. Stuff not useful or needed in our current lives. Storage units are for living in the future or living in the past. You are either holding on to stuff because of the memories or because you think you may need it one day. It's a costly way to keep excess "out of sight out of mind". Yet with the burden of the monthly expense, we doubt it strays too far from the mind.

The average cost of a 10 X 30-foot storage unit is $175 per month. Units become progressively more expensive as they increase in size or have added perks like climate control and security. A unit with security and climate control can run more than $350 per month. So, if you go for the "fully loaded" unit you are looking at spending $4,200 per year! From our experience, people typically do not clear out their unit after one year. Life gets in the way and they only think about it monthly when paying the bill. Years pass by. After five years you have then spent $21,000 on that fully loaded unit! Imagine what you could have used that money for: college tuition, a new car, an amazing European tour, the list is endless. Also, at that price tag how many times could you have replaced the items you are storing?

One of our clients jokingly had the idea of lighting a match and tossing it into the unit to rid herself of the burden of having to look through everything that she had been holding onto. Another client paid month after month because they were too paralyzed to think about the clearing-out process. For yet another, we were able to replace much of the existing furniture in their home and their children's homes with some of the beautiful antique pieces that had been stored for years. Not only were they relieved of the monthly storage expense, but they also made money by selling some of the furniture from the unit and their home. The process can be overwhelming but so freeing! Set a deadline and enlist the help of family, friends or hired professionals.

Tips:

1. Eliminate the junk and trash that cannot be sold or donated.

2. Always be mindful of The Four Simple Nest Questions:

> • Do I LOVE it and does it celebrate me?

> • Is it useful and functional on a regular basis (or have I worn it in the last year)?

• Can it serve another purpose in my home?

• Would I buy it again if I had the opportunity?

3. Any items that you are storing for your adult children need to be returned to them. If you are storing furniture for them for a later date, touch base with them and make sure they still want it. And if they do, agree on a deadline so that you are not carrying the expense longer than you need to.

4. Move all items out that can be donated. If you have a substantial amount, contact organizations like Habitat for Humanity, Good Will or the Salvation Army for pick up on site.

5. For items that can be sold, the same options apply as when going through your home: Take a picture of the item(s) and use a safe, social network site to market it for sale, visit a local antique market for dealer interest, contact a consignment shop to see if they are interested in selling it for you, splitting the profit.

For many of our clients who hire us to clear their unit, we have been able to sell or consign the items in storage giving them a nice profit to help pay for our services. Of course, items can also be donated to different community outreach programs to change the lives of those in need (see RESOURCES in the back of the book for a list of outreach ideas).

If you have a storage unit that is weighing you down, there is no time like the present to eliminate this stress from your life. Don't let your stuff hold you down and drain your wallet a month longer!

X. IN CASE OF EMERGENCY

The most important things in life aren't things.
-Anthony J. D'Angelo

Over the last few years Charleston, and many parts of the world, have been hit or at risk for a multitude of natural disasters. Loss of life and injury are the most devastating by-products of a storm, but even those who are blessed to walk away unscathed are often impacted in some way. From damage to the home and loss of personal property, to financial strain and power outages, the aftermath can be brutal. Whether we are forced to evacuate or choose to stay and "ride it out", one thing is certain - we are forced to assess the value we place on belongings. An imminent natural disaster really puts things into focus, especially if you are evacuating. We have had the unfortunate burden of being part of several evacuations and later discussed what material possessions we took with us.

Here is our list:

• Family pictures and home movies that cannot be replaced

• Favorite art pieces (this was tough, but we set a limit)

• Our children's memory boxes

• A small safe with important paperwork

• Valuable jewelry/sterling silver flatware

That was it. We came to the conclusion that everything else can be replaced. As you move forward simplifying your home, keep this question in the back of your mind "What would you take?". Having a disaster checklist in place ahead of oncoming weather is the key to reducing stress and insuring safety for your family.

Tips:

1. Make sure you have your homeowner's and flood (if applicable) insurance in place.

2. Have at least a 2-week supply of water and non-perishable food for each member of your family. Don't forget about your pets.

3. Have your First-Aid kit fully stocked and in a safe place.

4. Store a few large bins filled with heavy duty garbage bags and bubble wrap to protect the important contents of your home.

5. Take pictures or videos of every room in your home, along with important objects. Taking a video will allow you to narrate notable information.

6. Take pictures of receipts, model and serial numbers of appliances and larger items. For smaller, valuable items take pictures of receipts as well if you have them. Include any appraisals that have been done.

7. It is a good idea to purchase a small fireproof safe for all important paperwork i.e. original notes, wills, social security

and birth certificates, passports, warranties, receipts and appraisals. If you evacuate, a small safe is easy to carry along. A safe deposit box at your bank is also a great option.

8. Roll up rugs on the first level of your home if flooding is expected.

9. Move larger tables away from windows and place important objects on top.

10. Wrap art work, pictures and breakable treasures in bubble wrap, and place in bins with tops secured. Photo albums can be placed in garbage bags and placed in the bins. For larger art work, place in heavy duty garbage bags. Put art and bins in a inner closet or bathroom, off the floor.

11. Take pictures of pets just in case you are separated from them.

12. Have flashlights and extra batteries on hand.

13. Keep a bag of ice in your freezer should you loose power and need to move perishable items to a cooler. Make sure you have a cooler!

14. Make sure cars have a full tank of gas. Fill an extra gas can if evacuating in case you are in heavy traffic. Gas stations tend to run out of gas quickly when evacuations are imminent.

15. Fill your bathtubs with water.

16. Use the Penny in a Cup trick.

17. Be smart and have an evacuation plan in place. If it is recommended that your area evacuate be ready to go!

Penny in a cup: Put a cup of water in your freezer and freeze solid. Then put a penny (or any coin) on top of the frozen water and leave it in your freezer. Should you need to evacuate, you will be able to see if your food completely thawed and then refroze while you were gone or whether it stayed frozen. If the penny has fallen to the bottom of the cup, then all of the freezer food has defrosted and should be thrown out. But if the penny is either on the top or in the middle of the cup then your food may still be ok. But of course, if in doubt then throw it out! You can also use this technique if going on vacation. Just go ahead and freeze a cup of water now, add a penny and leave it in your freezer so you will always be ready!

Living simply not only makes the preparation of a potential storm easier, but it also allows for a safer aftermath. After the recent hurricanes, the amount of trash, debris and personal belongings that lined the streets of towns and cities affected was unreal. The horrific flooding resulted in a calamitous loss of personal property. It all had to be sorted through, disposed of, picked up by the sanitation department and then laid to rest in a landfill. Moving forward after such loss has made many re-think the amount of stuff they want to deal with. The number one goal is to make sure you and your family are safe. Don't put your life or the lives of emergency responders in danger because you want to protect your material possessions.

XI. EDIT BEFORE A MOVE

You should have nothing in your home that you do not know to be useful or believe to be beautiful.
-William Morris

A few years ago, Kari made a pretty drastic move for a family of five, plus a very large dog. They moved from their spacious home of 2400 square feet into a 1300- square-foot bungalow. After living in their home for 10 wonderful years, they decided it was time to change things up. It was a bittersweet decision. Kari was excited about being part of the renovation and revitalization of a 1950's home but challenged by what it would entail to get her family and their belongings into about half the space. Their goal was pretty clear. They wanted to simplify their lives so they could focus more on living and less on the upkeep and bills that go along with caring for a larger home. So, they took the leap.

After using our Simple Nest Process, they now have less stuff to manage and Kari and her family have the extra time they were all craving. Before, they felt like hamsters on a wheel with a never-ending to-do list. Yes, that list still exists, but it is smaller and easier to manage. They travel more, yard work is now a hobby instead of a burden, and cleaning the house takes no time at all. They have quality and quantity family time and this is what matters most to them.

Whether you are preparing to move to a smaller space or a larger space, it is a good time to take inventory of your things. Not only does a home that is clutter-free sell more quickly, releasing some of your baggage means less stuff to drag with you to your next home. Have you ever gotten ready to move and realized you still have unpacked boxes from the previous move? Moving is a time for a fresh start, so why take your excess baggage with you? De-cluttering before a move can be an intense process, so starting small and setting clear expectations is the key.

Tips:

1. Set the timer and focus your attention on one area (a closet, drawer, cabinet, etc.).

2. Stick to the allotted time to conserve your energy and don't get sidetracked!

3. Have five labeled bins:

- Keep
- Sell
- Donate
- Recycle
- Trash

4. Use The Four Simple Nest Questions as your guide:

- Do I LOVE it and does it celebrate me?
- Is it useful and functional on a regular basis (or have I worn it in the last year)?
- Can it serve another purpose in my home?
- Would I buy it again if I had the opportunity?

5. Do not move stuff that does not belong to you. If you have adult children and still have things that belong to them, or are storing items for a friend, now is the time to have them collect their stuff. Period.

6. Pass on, donate or recycle items before you change your mind.

7. Moving is stressful so you need all hands on deck! Include the entire family in the process.

Once you have slowly moved through your house de-cluttering every nook and cranny, it is time to donate the excess or have a huge yard sale or even an estate sale. If a yard sale or estate sale is the route you take, remember if it does not sell, it gets donated! Don't let it back in the house. The expense to move unnecessary items will be a financial burden and a waste of time and energy as you begin to unpack them in your new home. Take only the items you love and allow this move to be a new beginning for you and your family.

XII. STAGING YOUR HOME FOR SALE

Home is the comfiest place to be.
–Winnie the Pooh

One of the many fun aspects of our job is helping stage homes for sale. Our clients have received quick offers on their homes by letting us help them simplify first and then use what they already have to stage. Not only does it reduce the costs of their upcoming move but they know exactly what will be going with them to their new home. Investing the time upfront also saves time on the back-end when it is time to unpack. Being able to sell your home quickly reduces the stress of having your house on the market. If you have kids and have ever sold a home, you know what we are talking about! Keeping the house tidy and having to leave at a moment's notice due to a showing is a hard way to live for anyone, especially those with children and/or animals!

If you are getting ready to put your home on the market, it is vital that you take the time to stage it properly. A potential buyer needs to envision your home as their home. As they walk through, they need to be able to picture their color schemes, their furniture, and most importantly, their family in your space. To help buyers do this, you have to remove as much excess as possible. This means clearing out personal items like pictures, as well as extra furniture – all of which make a room look crowded. When your home looks and feels spacious, the potential homebuyer has the ability to move freely, with vision.

Tips:

1. Follow our Simple Nest Process to pare down to only what you will be moving with you.

2. Deep clean the whole house.

3. Make sure closets, pantry, cabinets and drawers are tidy because lookers will be peeking.

4. Toilet seats need to be down, shower curtains closed and fresh towels hung in the bathrooms. Clear off all personal items from bathroom counters. Create a "spa like" vibe.

5. Get rid of old doormats and worn rugs. Note: Removing certain area rugs in your home can open up and lighten a space.

6. Make sure your garage, attic, basement and yard are neat.

7. Welcome visitors with planters filled with pretty flowers on your front porch.

8. Remove, or at least limit the amount of artificial greenery and flowers in the house.

9. Have your green cleaner and a few rags on hand to quickly wipe down counters.

10. If you have pets, make sure you keep them groomed and clean to reduce animal aromas and shedding. Get rid of kitty

litter boxes for showings and pick up pet waste in the yard.

11. Do not use strong candles or air fresheners.

12. Clean with green cleaners. They have fresh, light scents.

13. Keep two baskets on hand. One to corral paperwork, kitchen and bathroom counter items. The other for laundry. Take these items with you when you have a showing.

14. If you have the time and can bare the expense, paint your walls a pretty neutral color. This makes it easier for your potential buyer to envision their style in your space. At the very least, using your current paint, touch up wall markings and patch and paint over nail holes.

Once your home is staged and all set to show, don't forget to add a personal touch. How about writing a letter to your future homebuyer? Make copies and leave them on your kitchen counter. If they are working with a realtor, they will have the MLS information that includes the details of your home, the schools zoned, if there are Home Owner Association dues and what not. What the potential buyer does not have are the intimate details regarding your home – what has made this house a home for you.

Here is a Sample Letter:

Thank you for coming to look at our home! The memories and friendships we have created in (neighborhood name) will last a life-time! From holiday parades and picnics in the neighborhood park, to the scrambled suppers, Bunco and book clubs, this neighborhood has something to offer everyone. Every age is represented here, from the newborn to the retiree, making our community fun, diverse and wonderful!

Our children have been able to step out of our front door and have a playmate on any given day. They can walk to the park, go fishing in the pond, play four-square in the driveway and "manhunt" in the evenings. Now that they are old enough, they can ride their bikes to our phenomenal elementary school and to the neighborhood pool for swim team practice in the summer.

Our house has been our home for (#) fabulous years. We hope as you walk through the rooms that you can picture your family gathering for dinner in the cozy dining room, cookouts with friends on the back porch, the laughter of children enjoying birthday parties in the backyard and warm summer nights sitting on the front porch swing.

There's a quote that says "Don't buy the house, buy the neighborhood". We wanted you to know how wonderful this neighborhood is so that you can make the best decision for you and your family.

Best,
The (last name) family

Taking the time to make sure your home is in tip top shape will increase your chances for a quick sale at a price you are happy with. Think about what is important to you when looking for a new house and let the potential buyer feel the good vibes of this home as they walk through.

XIII. WHAT WE LEAVE BEHIND

You'll never see a U-Haul behind a hearse.
-Denzel Washington

One of the hardest, but most rewarding parts of our job, is assisting clients who need help clearing out the house of a loved one who has passed. Making sure that the paperwork and contents of the home are properly cared for is both emotional and time consuming for the caretaker of the property who is no doubt trying to balance their own work and family life. Being charged with taking care of someone else's estate comes with many decisions and a whole lot of leg work, particularly if a plan has not been established beforehand.

This was the case when we were hired to empty the home of Beatrice after she mysteriously passed away. The project was just too daunting for the family, and they simply did not have the time to invest. Most of the contents in the house were relics from the prominent, downtown Charleston mansion that Beatrice once shared with her prestigious parents. She continued to live alone in the historic home long after their deaths.

When Beatrice moved into the new 4,000 square-foot home - two years before - she had never really unpacked. Floor-to-ceiling bags and boxes filled every room and garage. We scrupulously went through each bag and box retrieving fine linens, gemstones, rare coins, extravagant ball gowns, love letters and more. We would imagine fancy parties with men in black tails and women in long white gloves and beautiful gowns sipping champagne out of the beautiful crystal we had uncovered. But once again, we would ultimately rent a walk-in dumpster and sadly dispose of items ruined due to poor storage.

Our time spent in Beatrice's home had allowed us to learn about a woman that we never had the privilege of knowing. It also made us question whether we believe in ghosts. We could feel a sadness lurking in the house, as if Beatrice herself were watching us as we cleared away items that at one time had meant so much to her. Each morning we would enter the house and say good morning to Beatrice just because it made us feel better. We would find ourselves asking questions out loud hoping she would answer. Mostly we wondered what kind of life she had had while surrounded by garbage bags and boxes full of stuff.

We finished our project with a successful estate sale and a family that was immensely grateful for our services. Hiring us to clear Beatrice's home had given them the time they needed to handle the overwhelming paperwork involved with her estate and to continue with their own family and job responsibilities.

During the final days of the estate sale, we met the new owners of the house. Once they found out our profession, we were immediately hired to help them settle into their new home. We happily agreed and were excited that we could help bring new life into a house that we had grown to love. We walked the couple through the estate sale showing them items of historical significance that we had learned about from the antique dealers and appraisers hired to help us determine the provenance and pricing of the spectacular treasures uncovered in the house. We were also able to help the new owners decide on a few pieces to purchase that would serve as a special reminder of the incredible history of a distinguished Charleston family.

Any of our clients will tell you that when it comes to our work, we are very meticulous. We inspected Beatrice's house from top to bottom, more than once, before the new owners moved in to make sure not even a paper clip could be found. We received a call from the new owner on moving day letting us know that when opening the drawers in the master bathroom they discovered they were filled with Beatrice's hair brushes, toothpaste and soaps. Could we have missed her bathroom drawers? Let's just say that when clearing her bathroom days prior, we were able to donate to a local shelter a box full of new toothpaste, soaps and shampoos that had been stored in the master bath drawers. We think Beatrice had the final word.

This project taught us more than we could ever have imagined, and we are grateful for the experience. We learned first-hand that what we leave behind will indeed be dealt with by others. Trust us when we say that we never cease to be amazed by our findings! From empty liquor bottles hidden in attic corners and outside sheds to "adult play toys" and provocative pictures stashed in the backs of closets and drawers (and we find this a lot!), we've seen it all. We have cleared dumpster loads of trash, coordinated countless donation pickups, hosted estate sales, arranged for vendors to come in to purchase furniture and knick-knacks, and, at the end of the process, staged homes for sale. It is an emotional roller coaster for our clients. It is not only heartbreaking, but it is also preventable. Our stuff should never be someone else's burden.

The inevitable will happen, and good planning is vital. Having a life of simplicity will not only allow for a healthier and more freeing life style now, but it's a gift to those you leave behind.

Tips:

1. Have an up-to-date Last Will and Testament in place. This is vital and especially important if you have children under the age of 18. Guardianship needs to be established as well as trust funds if applicable. An estate attorney will be able

to guide you through the process and make sure pertinent details are covered. For situations less complicated, there are websites that provide online wills. Choose an executor for your estate and make sure that the he or she has a copy of your will or knows where it is located.

2. Ask your loved ones which of your treasures they would cherish. This is never an easy process, but it definitely will prevent any kind of bitterness and greed down the road. Have a list that you can include with your will.

3. Follow our Simple Nest Process and clear the clutter from your home!

4. Stay on top of important paperwork.

5. Include a list of important contacts with your Last Will and Testament i.e. life insurance agent, financial planner, attorney, etc.

6. If you have documents in a lock box within a financial

institution, make sure and include a list of those documents with your will (and also make sure someone knows where the keys to the lockbox are!).

The things we keep in our homes must be carefully considered. Is there anything you would not want others to discover? Though you will not be worrying about it when the time comes, just remember that what you leave behind will become part of their memory of you.

XIV. LIVING LIFE WITH INTENTION AND PURPOSE

The purpose of life is to live it, to taste experience to the utmost, to reach out eagerly and without fear for newer and richer experience.

-Eleanor Roosevelt

There are circumstances in life that we cannot control. What we can control however, is how much stuff we have, what we spend our money on, and how we care for the earth. As we begin to simplify, our lives will come into focus. We see that acquiring stuff is not what makes us happy and is certainly not what defines us. As the burden of having to manage our stuff goes away, we will find balance and peace while giving back to the world.

One of the most important gifts that we can give to the next generation is to show them how to manage life - not materialism. We must emphasize to our children that identity is not found in how many trophies and certificates we receive, how many advanced placements we qualify for, or the titles we hold in the jobs we have the privilege of working in.

Identity is found in our faith and our character. It is found in hard work versus instant gratification. It is found in the memories we make and not in the things we obtain. It is found in valuing our planet and the people on it. Identity is found when we live with intention and purpose because in finding our purpose, we discover how best to serve.

There is no first-place ribbon for being busy, and it is true that life can pass you right by while you are busy planning for the future. Recognize that time is the one thing that we can never get back and begin spending the gift of another day acknowledging who and what you love, being grateful, serving people and protecting our environment.

As Woodrow Wilson once said, "You are here in order to enable the world to live more amply, with greater vision, with a finer spirit of hope and achievement. You are here to enrich the world."

There will always be challenges, but stay the course,

keep this book handy and remember, in everything, to pause. Our hope is that you take the time to breathe, discover your most peaceful selves and create your own simple nest.

Cheers,

Liz and Kari

XV. RESOURCES AND MORE TIPS

PASS IT ON – DONATE!

Being able to help others with your excess when paring down and simplifying your life is an amazing byproduct of this process! Keep this idea in mind when determining what to keep and what to let go, and it may help to make the decision easier. Research local organizations in your community that you feel passionate about, below is a list of local and national charities close to our hearts.

- Habitat for Humanity
- Goodwill
- Salvation Army
- Halos

- East Cooper Community Outreach

- Lowcountry Orphan Relief

- Operation Give

- Dress for Success

- Soles 4 Souls

- The Glass Slipper Project

- Ronald McDonald House

- Global Literacy Project

- Knots of Love

- Bicycles for Humanity

- Mr. Holland's Opus Foundation

- National Kidney Foundation

- Purple Heart

- UNICEF

- Make-A-Wish Foundation

- Animal Shelters

- My Sister's House

- Vehicles for Veterans

- Saint Vincent De Paul

EARTH FRIENDLY TIPS TO ———————— REDUCE YOUR MAIL

1. Decrease your mail by requesting paperless billing and pay bills online.

2. Catalogchoice.org makes it easy to eliminate catalogs, credit card solicitations, and more.

3. Go to the online source (the company website) and request to be removed from their list. This is also a good way to remove yourself from their email subscription list as well.

Important Documents-

What to Keep and For How Long:

- Loan Documents - Keep until the loan is paid off.
- Car Titles – Keep until you sell the car.
- Property Deeds – Keep until property is sold.
- Stocks, bonds, mutual funds – Keep purchase confirmations until you sell the investments.
- Birth and Death Certificates, Marriage Licenses, Divorce Decrees, Social Security Cards, Military

Discharge Papers, Estate Planning Documents, Life Insurance Policies – Keep forever!

• Monthly or quarterly investment statements - Shred once new ones arrive.

• Social Security statements – Shred once new ones arrive.

• Annually renewed insurance policies – Shred once new ones arrive.

• Credit card receipts- Shred once you've reconciled them with your monthly statement unless it's needed for a warranty or tax filing. In those situations, keep the receipts with the manual until the warranty expires or with your tax paperwork.

• Bank deposit or withdrawal slips – Shred once you reconcile with your monthly statement.

• Credit card/bank statements - 7 years if needed for tax purposes, otherwise one year.

• Annual investment statements - Until you sell the investments, then hold them for 7 years after you sell with your tax papers.

• Paycheck stubs - After reconciling with your W-2

form and have paid your taxes.

• Health Explanation of Benefits/Medical Records

  - 1 year.

• Taxes and supporting records (e.g., tax-related

medical bills, donations, etc.). Keep for 7 years.

(For more information visit www.irs.gov as well as

www.consumerreports.org)

PREVENTING FOOD WASTE ──────

In our experience, the number one reason for food waste is due to expiration dates. Cluttered pantries, where items get lost and forgotten, are usually the culprit. The best solution to prevent overstocking our shelves is to focus on weekly planning. Try to avoid any "bulk" shopping unless you know for sure it will be eaten or used. Scan your pantry weekly and if you see something on the verge of expiring, or you know you are not going to eat it, either use it or donate it to your local food bank ASAP!

Tips For Successful Weekly Shopping:

1. Plan a breakfast menu for one week. Take into consideration

the number of people in your family so you don't run out of food before the next shopping trip. Store cereals in clear jars so that you know when you are running low. (How many times have you reached for a box of cereal only to find its contents empty?) Oatmeal and smoothies, made with frozen fruit, are also great options for nutritious and delicious breakfasts.

2. Plan lunches for one week. Whether just for you, or lunchbox items for kids, mix it up a bit. Make sure you have enough luncheon meats, breads/crackers, yogurt, fruits and veggies to last for that week. If you buy sandwich meat with no preservatives, remember it will only last about 3-4 days. After that, plan to pack items like peanut butter (or other spreads) sandwiches or crackers, veggies, fruits and pretzels with cheese or hummus, etc. that will work until your next shopping trip.

3. Plan snacks for one week. Maybe throw a couple of homemade goodies in there (which means that you will have to make sure you have the ingredients). Again, use clear jars for pretzels, crackers and other snacks that will be put in the

pantry. It's a great way to monitor how much is eaten during the week and alerts you when you run out. Then, you can adjust next week's list accordingly.

4. For dinner, plan a menu for the first 2-3 nights using fresh meats and fish, fruits and veggies. For nights 4-7 buy grains, pastas, frozen veggies and meats that can be frozen.

5. Unless you do a lot of baking, it is best to buy smaller bags of flour and sugars. Watch for the expiration dates on all of your baking products. Keep in large Ziploc bags that you can label with their expiration dates or empty into labeled glass containers and record the expiration date in pencil on the label (that way you can erase the date and put a new date in when you replenish). Also, watch for the expiration dates of your spices. They will lose their zeal and foods will not get the benefit of the spice.

6. A note about the fridge: Dairy products can be tricky. Depending on how much milk your family drinks, or how much room you have in your fridge, will determine whether

you need to make an additional trip to the market that week. Be careful not to overbuy in the milk and egg department. Those items expire too and there is nothing worse than spoiled milk!

7. Try to restrain from going to the store and see what you can make work for the rest of the week based on what you have in your pantry, fridge and freezer. It is amazing what you can create! Whether grilled cheese and tomato soup or breakfast for dinner, try and hold out until your next weekly market trip. You will be amazed at the money saved on groceries! And, with the money saved, you can treat your family to a night out and enjoy a break from the kitchen!

HOW TO DISPOSE OF UNUSED AND/OR —— HARMFUL MEDICATIONS PROPERLY

National Prescription Drug Take-Back Events – This is the FDA preferred method of getting rid of unused prescriptions drugs. If you do not have access to a take-back event or prescription drop-off - mix medicines (do not crush tablets or capsules) with a substance such as dirt, cat litter, or used coffee grounds; and place mixture in a sealed container before throwing in the trash. Some medications are recommended for disposal by flushing when take-back options are not readily available. According to the FDA "when it isn't possible to return these medicines through a take-back program or to a DEA-authorized collector via a collection box or mail-back program, consumers should flush them down the toilet to immediately and permanently remove this risk from their home. Reducing the risk of harm from accidental exposure to this small, select list of medicines is of utmost concern to FDA and we believe that this risk far outweighs any potential risk to human health or the environment that may come from disposal by flushing. FDA continues to work with and encourage manufacturers of these medicines to develop alternative, safe disposal systems."

Medications to be flushed if a collection program is unavailable:

- Benzhydrocodone
- Acetaminophen
- Buprenorphine

- Fentanyl

- Diazepam

- Hydrocodone

- Hydromorphone

- Meperidine

- Methadone

- Methylphenidate

- Morphine

- Oxycodone

- Oxymorphone

- Tapentadol

- Sodium Oxybate

FIRST-AID KITS

The American Red Cross website is a great resource for making sure you have all that you need should an emergency occur – even if it's just a scraped knee. In addition to your supplies, make sure to include a list of emergency contact numbers. You should have a first-aid kit in your home and in each of your vehicles. The Red Cross recommends the below items (for a family of four) be in your kit. You

can also purchase a fully stocked first-aid kit online from the
Red Cross.

- 2 absorbent compress dressings (5 x 9 inches)
- 25 adhesive bandages (assorted sizes)
- 1 adhesive cloth tape (10 yards x 1 inch)
- 5 antibiotic ointment packets (approximately
1 gram)
- 5 antiseptic wipe packets
- 2 packets of aspirin (81 mg each)
- 1 blanket (space blanket)
- 1 breathing barrier (with one-way valve)
- 1 instant cold compress (note: we suggest several
compresses for active families)
- 2 pair of nonlatex gloves (size: large)
- 2 hydrocortisone ointment packets (approximately
1 gram each)
- Scissors
- 1 roller bandage (3 inches wide)
- 1 roller bandage (4 inches wide)
- 5 sterile gauze pads (3 x 3 inches)
- 5 sterile gauze pads (4 x 4 inches)

- Oral thermometer (non-mercury/non-glass)

- 2 triangular bandages

- Tweezers

- First aid instruction booklet

- Water

- Flash Light with working batteries

- Personal items such as prescription medications

Note: Frequently check the supplies in your first-aid kit and replenish as needed.

TIPS ON TRAINING THE MIND ──────

Studies have shown remarkable health benefits from practicing techniques that train the mind. Choosing the method that works best for you is personal. We encourage you to explore different methods to discover what truly resonates with you. This will help to clear the mental clutter and train your mind to pause. Listed below are our favorite techniques to quiet the mind.

Prayer:

The power of prayer can be a very healing practice. Through faith, we find courage, support and cleansing by talking to and trusting in God. Learning to turn over those worries and concerns that could otherwise consume our mind and heart can bring us the strength we need to face each day. In addition, being able to offer prayers of thanksgiving for the good things in our lives allows us to recognize those blessings that can easily be taken for granted.

Yoga:

Yoga comes from the Sanskrit root yuj, which means "to join" or "to yoke". Creating a sense of harmony for the body, mind and spirit. Not only do we benefit physically from the practice of Yoga but Asana, the physical practice of Yoga, is a moving meditation, which calms the mind. Within the Yoga Sutras, the ancient text of Yoga, the second sutra states Yogas Citta Vritti Nirodhah - meaning restrain the waves of the mind. If the water is wavy, you can't see the bottom of the sea. If there is stillness, there is clarity and you can discover the treasure. Whether we are practicing asana or meditation restraining the "waves of the mind" is the ultimate goal.

Meditation:

According to the Oxford Dictionary, to meditate is to focus one's mind for a period of time, in silence or with the aid of chanting, for religious or spiritual purposes or as a method of relaxation. The goal of meditation is to guide the mind to a state of quiet stillness. Unfortunately, learning to meditate cannot be checked off the list like running a marathon, it ebbs and flows throughout one's lifetime. There will be times where sitting for thirty seconds will be utter torture and other times where you can sit peacefully for 20 minutes with ease. We might never get it perfect but regardless the rewards are great.

Journaling:

Writing down our thoughts on paper can free our mind and prevent brain overload. We are then able to make sense of our thoughts, dreams, ideas and worries and determine how to move forward. Getting into the habit of keeping pen and paper at hand throughout the day, and by our bed at night, allows us to jot down those mental notes that seem impossible to recall later on. Below is a list of types of journaling to explore:

- Gratitude – a daily list of positive things/experiences
- Bullet - quick thoughts, notes, lists
- Dream – a record of dreams
- Spiritual – a record of one's spiritual journey
- Gardening/Nature - notes on your experience in nature, plants you discover while exploring, the progress of your personal garden
- Planning - planting seeds for the future, places to see, people to connect with, experiences to look forward to
- Creativity – inspiring ideas and visions

COMPOSTING 101

Pick a Container - Bin, Pile, or a Tumbler. The size and type of container that you will use for composting will depend on how much space you have and how much waste your family will produce. If you have a large yard, you can have a large system that can accommodate grass clippings, leaves and food waste. Those tight on space, and who produce less organic waste, can use a tumbler or smaller container.

What to Compost:

- Vegetable and fruit scraps

- Grass clippings

- Leaves

- Shredded newspaper

- Paper products

- Coffee grounds

- Egg shells

- Cardboard paper

- Saw dust

- Twigs and small branches

- Tea bags

How to Create a Successful Compost Pile:

Turn your pile on a regular basis. If you have a tumbler this is an easy task. With a pile or smaller container use a garden fork to turn it weekly. This will encourage the break-down of organic matter. Moisture level should be equal to a "wrung out sponge". If your pile is too moist, add leaves, paper and other items to soak up moisture. If it is too dry, add more scraps and plant-based items.

Finished Product: Once your compost resembles a dark rich soil you can then use it in your vegetable garden and planters.

BE CREATIVE AND REPURPOSE! ─────────

Warning: once your creative genes begin to flow, you may find your weekends are full of fun projects! There is an exhilarating sense of accomplishment when you turn something ordinary into something grand! You save money by repurposing versus buying something new and you also save money when you do it yourself. Give yourself a little credit, you can do it!

Chalk Paint:

Chalk paint is all the rage and is one of the easiest ways to transform a piece of furniture. There many brands of chalk paint available due to its popularity. Our favorite continues to be Annie Sloan. She is the original mastermind behind chalk paint and her work is such an inspiration. We have transformed many pieces of furniture with chalk paint that otherwise would have been out the door if it were up to our clients. The technique is easy and, with an array of colors and color mix ideas, there is no reason that even the amateur artist could not take a drab piece of brown furniture and turn it into a work of art! Plus, chalk paint works on lamp bases, fabric, picture frames, flower pots, floors, kitchen cabinets and more!

Refinish:

It may take the level of difficulty up a notch, but the rewards of refinishing a piece of furniture outweigh the hardship (and really, it is not that hard). Visit your local hardware store and talk to a professional about the tools and products you will need for your project. Of course, you can always find a multitude of YouTube videos on the subject as well. Whether you want to completely strip a piece and re-stain it or sand it down and then just oil it well, breathing new life into a beautiful piece of furniture has a satisfaction all of its own.

How wonderful to continue to pass down the history of a

family treasure – whether it is your family's history or not!

Give it a New Responsibility:

Furniture and items in our home, though made for a certain purpose originally, can be promoted to a new role. We mentioned some ideas in HEIRLOOMS AND THE FINER THINGS. Again, silver trays can be separated from tea sets and used on coffee tables and even your bathroom vanity. The silver teapot and coffee pot can be used as a vase for flowers or to corral kitchen utensils. Chest of drawers can move from the bedroom to a foyer or kitchen to store linens, china and more. Or, if you have a chest of drawers that you are not using, take the drawers out, paint them if you want, attach wheels to the bottom four corners, change the handle if necessary, and use for under bed storage! This creates a great home for gift-wrap, blankets and toys. There are so many ideas that you can come up with to repurpose the unused items in your home. Of course, if you do not need it, cannot benefit from its use or flat out do not like it, then let it go!

LIVING LOCAL ─────────────────────

Supporting local business owners, artisans and eateries has always been a priority for us. Not only does it benefit the economy, but it helps to preserve the environment - as the small business owner will be more inclined to use existing buildings to set up shop as opposed to tearing down to rebuild or finding green space to clear and build on. Eat, shop and play local and watch your community thrive!

Eat Local:

Shopping at the farmers markets is a great way to enjoy the simplicity of farm-to-table cuisine while meeting the growers of your family's food. The benefits of buying local reach even further.

1. Conserving fossil fuels - much of the food in grocery stores travels thousands of miles to reach its destination. Buying locally significantly reduces the impact on the environment.

2. Taste - Buying freshly picked/seasonal food just tastes better! It has not sat on a truck or in a grocery store for days or weeks losing valuable flavor and nutrients.

3. Access to organic non-GMO fruits and vegetables - Most farmers markets offer reasonably priced organic food.

4. Quality time - A fun and productive way to get some vitamin D and spend time with family and friends.

5. Builds a strong community - Supports the local economy and local family farms.

Whether you live in the city, country or suburbs, chances are there are several farmers markets in your area. Local Harvest (localharvest.org) is a great resource to learn more about markets near your home and wherever you may travel.

Shop Local:

Supporting local shops and markets have many benefits. Not only does it organically promote community, but it strengthens the local economy. Here are a few of our favorite reasons to shop small and local:

1. Creates jobs.

2. Your tax dollars stay within your community.

3. Small businesses are known for directly giving back to the community.

4. Receive top-notch customer service while getting to know your neighbors.

Play Local:

Entertainment comes in many forms, so when deciding what to do in your free time consider local first! Support local theatre and take in a show, pack a picnic and head to your favorite park, plan family field trips to explore the history of your city or town and dine in local restaurants – chances are, most of them are supporting the local farmers in your community!

Made in the USA
Columbia, SC
10 February 2021